"Krumbz

Letters to inmate #355-188

"Krumbz"

Letters to inmate #355-188

The motivational and inspirational

Letters to Grady McCain from

Idriis Bilaal

Foreword by: Tamika "Meek Love" Diggs

Grady McCain, June 29th 1971

"Krumbz" Letters to inmate #355-188/

Foreword by: Tamika "Meek Love" Diggs;

Introduction by: Grady McCain

© 2013 by Grady McCain

ISBN 978-1-304-02812-9

Printed in the United States of America

Contents

Grady L. McCain

(June 29th, 1971)

My name is Grady Leonard Lewis McCain, father of seven children (six daughters and one son), and the son of a deceased police officer (Robert McCain) and a mentally and physically abused woman (Vivian McCain). I was born on June 29th 1971 in N.W. Washington, D.C. at Sibley Hospital and was raised in between Takoma Park, Maryland and N.W. Washington D.C. I spent most of my time growing up playing, fighting, gambling, hustling, chilling, and learning the logics and rules of the streets in "Belford Towers", what I consider to be the largest projects in the state of MD. Here is where I obtained the character to survive any situation that I would find myself in throughout the course of my life.

I started selling drugs shortly after I graduated from High Point High School. The first strip (place where drugs are sold) that I ever hustled on was "Fort Totten

Drive" located in N.W. Washington D.C. near the Fort Totten bus and subway station off of Riggs Road. I hustled on many strips in Maryland and D.C. until I eventually graduated to selling "weight" (large amounts) and didn't have to stand on a strip any longer. At this time, I started hustling off of my pager and delivering large amounts of drugs all over the DMV. I sold Coke, Crack, Weed, PCP, and Ecstasy. I even started numerous self owned businesses during this time - selling everything from music, DVD's, and clothes, to my professional services to other companies.

I continued to sell drugs for 18yrs of my life until I was snitched on and set up by a fellow drug dealer/rapper from N.W. Washington D.C. I got hit with numerous gun and drug charges. I fought these charges in court for the next eleven months. When everything was said and done in the court room, I ended up with 15yrs, all suspended but 7yrs, first five mandatory without possibility of parole. I ended up only doing 3yrs and 10 months in jail and 3½ months on house arrest. Not bad for getting caught with drugs, money, 7 guns, and not snitching on anyone! I was blessed beyond my comprehension to just do almost

4yrs for what I got caught with. I could have EASILY got sentenced to 25yrs Fed time or better for the charges that I had. I guess there is a bigger plan meant for me.

This was the very first time in my lengthy criminal career that I had to do jail time. I had been locked up before and had caught charges before, but I had always beat my charges or been convicted and ended up with just probation. Never ever did I have to do a "Bid" (lengthy prison sentence)! The anxiety that I felt when I heard the judge read my sentence made me feel like Neo (Keanu Reeves) in the movie "The Matrix" when he threw up and then passed out after being told that the world had been destroyed and he had been plugged into a machine his entire life stuck in a dream state! I did not handle hearing my sentence well at all. Being led to the court room dungeon while looking back at my wife and children was heart wrenching. The beginning of my bid was very hard on me physically, emotionally, and mentally. I was so stressed out and anxious that I could not eat, sleep, or think in a constructive manner at all. My weight fell off of me; I lost 60lbs by the time I reached the prison where I would be serving out my sentence! I was slowly killing myself. I also was at risk of putting myself in harm's way because I wasn't on point in a dangerous environment. The worst thing I was going through was missing my children; seeing and also knowing what kind of pain that I was putting them through was very hard on me. The pain on their faces when they came to see me was a punishment all of its own separate from the punishment the state gave me.

Several convicts reached out to me and did their best to teach me the logics of bidding and the mind frame that I needed to be in to survive during this hellish period of my life that I found myself in. The love that I was shown from these special people was much needed, and I would like to take this time to thank all of them for the time they invested in me. The teachings that stood out and impacted me the most though, came from outside the prison in the form of letters. These letters taught, inspired, motivated, and informed me in a way that no other person was achieving for me. These letters also helped me to pass my time because I would have to read them over and over again to catch what he was trying to say. I had never experienced a person with such a unique vocabulary, unique way of thinking, and unique way of expressing their points and thoughts.

This person is an elderly man by the name of Idriis "Sweet P" Bilaal. In this book, I will share with you the thoughts, teachings, opinions, motivational speaking, and comfort that this man gave to me in the form of letters.

"KRUMBZ"

Letters to inmate #355-188

FOREWORD

Sentenced to 15 years in prison away from his wife and children, like every other person standing at the mercy of a judge, Grady McCain was suddenly ripped away from what was once his reality. The liberties he once had and the freedoms he previously enjoyed were suddenly taken away from him. The upcoming moments of watching his newborn son grow and the present moments of watching his daughters play became treasures that he would no longer have. Knowing that he was about to lose everything that he had up to that point in his life was about to become a harsh reality. Initial feelings of sickness, claustrophobia, anxiety, and culture shock would soon be Grady's new reality and thoughts of missing his children and not trusting his wife would soon lead him into a deep depression. Not accepting his reality would be one of many challenges that he faced during the beginning of his sentence.

For the sake of his health, Grady would soon have to learn how to accept and cope with his current reality. The outside world was no longer a part of his new reality inside of the four walls of prison. By developing relationships with a select few individuals in prison, he was educated with the knowledge that would soon lead him to mental stability. He learned mental and emotional discipline. He was taught to separate himself from the outside world; a world that he could no longer control. Grady gained strength and guidance through listening and applying what he learned from inmates, self help classes, and books. His focus to survive became his peace of mind, control of his thoughts, and taking better care of his health.

Although most of his relationships with friends and family on the outside were the cause of his mental and emotional problems, there were few exceptions. There was a relationship with one person in particular that did give Grady the hope and the support that he so desperately needed. In this book, you will see how Grady's life was positively impacted and turned around during his prison sentence through the power of words. These words served as his motivation, encouragement, joy, and peace. These words came from Idriis Bilaal, a business acquaintance and friend from the outside world.

As a teacher of the Quran, Idriis spent a lot of time in prisons teaching inmates. He encouraged Grady to seek God and read. Idriis also spent his time traveling from city to city, state to state and country to country. While doing so, he would send Grady letters and post cards of motivation. These letters served as moments of laughter, focus, and inspiration. Each letter had different effects on Grady's thoughts. The two would write and share their thoughts with each other for the first three years of Grady's prison sentence until Idriis fell on challenging times when his house was burned to the ground. The collection of letters and post cards have been compiled into this work entitled "Krumbz - Letters to Inmate #355-188". You will find that these letters are very unique. Idriis has his own language. Grady would spend a lot of his time just trying to figure out what Idriis was trying to say. Grady would compare these letters to bread crumbs found on a trail, but only leading to a better understanding of life and a peace of mind instead of a physical location. As you pick up these pieces (crumbs), you will find that each piece has a purpose, when all put together to form the finished puzzle, a source of inspiration and motivation will be the completed picture.

Tamika "Meek Love" Diggs   2013

"KRUMBZ"

Letters to inmate #355-188

"KRUMBZ"

Letters to inmate #355-188

Second, is one second shorter…Joy comes in the morning, when is morning? Everything happens for a reason, maybe to give us time to reflect on what and how we are doing. What we do, we do! Remain strong. "Krumbz"

Idriis "Sweet P"

Post card sent from Alabama on 6/25/09

Hi Grady (Mac), Idriis (Sweet P) here. Stay strong, nothing's bigger than Allah (God). Your cuz (Lady C) and I just returned from the "Big Easy" (New Orleans). Had a nice time, Essence Festival, maybe 800,000 people from all walks of life all shapes, sizes, Hughes (color) all getting along, funning, u know, "having fun". I'm trying to go back for the Louis Armstrong Festival on the 30th of July 2009. I like to drive, takes about 17-20 hours to drive. Take 95 South to Petersburg, then 85 to Atlanta, on to Montgomery Ala. then into the "Big Easy" (N.O.).

Hope you are finding something to do these days to enhance your mind. Maybe a search for fresh minds could be a good venture. In all things seek Allah (God) the creator, by any name is the same. The mind is the standard of an individual (Man/Woman). Most other parts of a human is Temporal, the mind ought to be to be in constant growth. Time is relative, compared to what? Is measurement of how far the travel has been, and so it is constant, therefore this too shall pass. We should try to prepare for the future. (Time) is there!

Anything I can do for you? Please don't hesitate to howlow (holla)! Lady C (Cheryl) is in contact with your family. She can give you a report. If you can make arrangements, I will visit you. I taught Islam there every Sunday from 1985-1990. I was teaching for the

Anne Arundel Community College. That was 20yrs ago. See how time goes!!! Stay strong. Stay focused. Free your mind! We'll pray for you and your family. Allah grant you peace of mind, it'll be all right! Peace and love!

Idriis Bilaal

Post card sent from Florida on 7/26/09

Peace/Blessings
God is God, all the time. Stay strong! Just somewhere
I've been (Fla.). Praying for u daily (even hourly) every
day is a day less. Remain strong as when last we met!
Peace!

Idriis

OYSTERS BIENVILLE

2	tablespoons butter	2	dozen oysters
1/4	cup shallots	1/3	cup seasoned bread
1/4	cup chopped parsley		crumbs
2	tablespoons flour	1/4	cup grated Parmesan
1	cup warm cream		cheese
1	cup bottled clam juice		Paprika and black pepper
2	egg yolks		Lemon wedges
1/3	cup white wine		
1/2	cup chopped shrimp		
1/2	cup chopped mushrooms		

Sauté shallots and parsley in butter until tender. Over low heat, add flour and whisk well to smooth out the lumps. Slowly stir in the cream and then the liquid. In a separate bowl, beat the egg yolks with the wine. Add shrimp and mushrooms and stir into the sauce. Season with pepper to taste. Cook over low heat until mixture thickens. Place oysters on half shells or on a layer of crumbs and ladle sauce over oysters. Sprinkle with a topping of breadcrumbs, cheese and dust with paprika. Shells are usually baked in a shallow pan of rock salt in a 400-degree oven for 30-30 minutes or until golden brown. Serve with lemon wedges. Serves 4.

Post card sent from New Orleans on 8/2/09

Greetings from the Big Easy, New Orleans! Take a little chill here. Hope U R doing well and holding on. Would be happy to visit U if possible. Again if I can do something to help, let me know.

Idriis "Sweet P"

8/8/09

As Salaam Alaikum
I wish peace unto you and all who are near you. I
returned from South Carolina via New Orleans, La.
Today and your letter was one of the most important
correspondences I found in/are among my mail.
Happy to sense that you are able to maintain strength,
stay strong, it's temporary, and comparatively short.
You have an important reason to hold, (family) a goal.
Rewards, benefits lie at the end of the journey, Nelson
Mandella (Rember) remember? Life has mountains and
valleys; one is only able to recognize mountains,
because of valley. Without darkness how can we know
light? All things must be measured in terms of the
creator, God, Allah, what of however one chooses to
refer to him, or "The Force". Allah blesses those who
have sincere concern for family. Especially children,
one's own children. You are person who cares for his
own reproduction (children). Allah will guide, direct U
in the proper way, his way. As long as U focus on what
Allah allowed U to reproduce. (Kids) He will C U
through.

I taught at Jessup (The Cut) from 1983-1987. I was
teaching Arabic and the Quran, every Sunday morning
from 9 to 12 noon. I was hired to teach there by
Arundel Community College in Annapolis, Md. That
was a very enjoyable experience. Do U listen to radio
there? WPFW FM 89.3 is recommended if you have

access. Do U want one? I can get U one, if U want one. Let me know.

Although I practice Islam, I just enjoyed an extremely high-spirited Revival (5 days) at a Baptist church, " Cedar Group Baptist Church" in Chester County S.C. about 25 miles south of Charlotte N.C. The revival was from August 2nd thru 6th of 2009. There is one God, Allah or Jesus, name calling. An apple by any name tastes the same. What price da Krumbz? Hit do what hit do

I have Verizon telephone service. I don't know what T-Netix is. Verizon should work, call me anytime. My cell is sprint, won't work, stay strong. As Salaam Alaikum "Peace"

Idriis "Sweet P"

8/12/09

What up Grady. (Sweet P) here. A beautiful day today!
All of them R for real. Bring-brought from such a long
way, that I now consider every moment a blessing
within itself. So hold strongly to the rope of hope,
future hope, faith and patience. Rome wasn't built in a
day. Total life involves bitter and sweet. Must
experience one to know the other (recognize the
other). Dream-should have dreams too-son-dreams
(they) can become realities truths, someone must bring
(speak) truth to the youth. Truth frees minds. Truth
reveals hope. Hope breathes the future. What price da
Krumbz? Hit do what hit do, waste not your time,
improve your mind. Mind is the standard of a man.
Man means mind, male or female. With me the search
is on for fresh minds. Where to find, in the Universe
(Earth)? Hard to find, always (too often) the other
kind. (Stale), unable to absolve, knowledge or
experiences. Like air, the mind must be free to explore.
Exploration is the key to education.

It's tight, but it is right to know better is to do better,
compared to what? To do better one must first have a
point of reference. Where is one coming from? Fret
not; Allah (God) has your back. The creator meets our
needs through his creatures (man, for us). Islam
teaches Zakat (charity) in great measures. Must (got to
) give to live.

As Salaam Alaikum! Peace to you
Who needs peace? Who doesn't? We all need peace.
Peace can be found within us. When at peace, sleep
comes easy. Good relationship with family brings
peace. One God, one purpose, peace for all. (Mankind)
(Kind of men)

Viva (Latin for life/live) Viva Vive, live life as it ought
to be lived. Revival is a derivative of Viva. So to be
revived is to be restarted, or brought back to the right
way of living. Allah (God) revived us, now, bless us
and give (grant) us peace. Peace in this world and in
the next and all Plato's of the journey. (Journey)
Krumbz

Idriis Bilaal "Sweet P" Peace!!!!

8/17/09

Still hotel hopping…investigating different hotels. This Holiday express near Charlotte, N.C. is attractive; it's just a few miles from both Charlotte and Rock Hill, small, compact somewhat. However, it has all things I need and I am accumulating points (rewards) which may be converted and used at other hotels like the Hilton, Ritz-Carlton, Gaylord (National Harbor). Free your mind, your standard. Once your mind is free, time is time and constant, so that what may seem forever time, before merely a passing moment in _time_. Hope, purpose, and family, these things make time easier to pass under discomforting times (Era's). One day, we're all going to be free for real! When you and all can or will be home with your families, which I know is your strongest wish. Soon and very soon, it will all be over. Keep or stay strong, obey those appointed over you. Perhaps the good intentions in you + the facts that U R a family concerned man, Allah (God) may intervene and negotiate your freedom. Keep a clean record. If possible, remain alone; only be with those that it is necessary to B with. Read, read, read, and then READ, Bible, Quran, any other books of God's guidance. Ascertain that is it is from God. Check the Authors of what U read.

"Sweet P" Idriis

8/17/09

I'm here for a Revival meeting at a church in S.C. Revival=Re, to do again, i.e. re-new, re-store, retrain, so revive, Latin for revive/relive-Viva La France Viva Viagra (LOL) (Smile), so a revival should restore life (viva/vive) to those who attend. One should leave a revival, revived! Rejuvenated, sorta a diff. individual, diff. out looks on things, more Godly, humble, kind, showing concern for fellow creatures or Allah's creation. Be mindful of the ant. Kill not, what U can create not. Killing is unauthorized by Allah. Love, help, support, show mercy, that's what a revived person should demonstrate. Tight but right! Humble ourselves before the creator (Allah). Show respect to all creation of HIS. Humbleness is pertinent. Valuable U make it one of your practices. Humbling, humbleness. Krumbz. Let not your mind B troubled for long, trouble is temporal, i.e. mountains vs. valleys. We must experience both. One refers the other.

Idriis Bilaal "Sweet P"

8/17/09

What's up Grady,
I'm presently in Fort Mill, S.C. 15 miles South of
Charlotte, N.C. I'm just hotel hopping. Trying to
combine some points, 10 points per dollar spent. Meet
lot of people, mostly business people. Those with
business smart. I'm basically in search of fresh minds.
That doesn't mean that the minds I am presently
involved with are stale, just not new or fresh. Fresh
minds fresh ideas. Keeping to man things, the main
things. Tight but right!

Cheryl may have mentioned to you the incident with
me in the "Big Easy". Minor, one must stay strong
under all circumstances. When one has family that
motivates, them, it's easy to be strong. Keeping hope
alive, that's no jive. Family, and that's your focus,
family and you were and still are a family orientated
person. So God will bless both U and your family.
Mistakes are made by all people. It should not mark
the end. The creator (Allah) rewards the family
concerned people, even when they error. Walk
strongly (Spiritually). Hold your head high! God first,
family second.

As I said, I have been hotel hopping for a few weeks,
became a member of the Priority Club, they have some
8-10 hotels in their chain, and each night spent in one
of them equal + amount of points. Today I'm in a

Holiday Xpress near Charlotte, N.C. We are planning a cruise in November. I've never been on a cruise. I've crossed the Atlantic Ocean some 6 or 7 times in a military ship, not like a luxury cruise, so that should be interesting. Do U have much access to learning? Learn all U can about any and everything. Study too the word of Allah (God), both Bible and Quran. U will or U may find a lot of similarities. Same God same people, Adam, Enoch (Idriis) Isacc (Izhak) Abraham (Ibrihaam) Isaac, Jacob (Yakub) Joseph (Yusuf) same persons, one heaven (Jardin) Garden. Everyone wants to go to heaven, no one ready or wants to die! Death really marks not the end, but the beginning, if nothing that a fresh beginning. Die to live, die that one might live a different and perhaps a better life. What price da Krumbz? Hit do what hit do. Dedicate thy (heart) your mind to knowledge, Learn, learn, learn, then study. Travel see what all has happened before your time, or our times.

Is any form of spiritual guidance provided there now? As I mentioned before, I taught Islam and Arabic there at Jessup from 1983 thru 1988 every Sunday for 3 hours. Some who attended the classes were released early with our recommendations. Others who study with other religious orders were also released early sometimes. So use this time to improve your mind and perhaps time spent there will be more rewarding. I.e. try turning all things to good. Beneficially, free your mind with knowledge/experiences. That's life. One must think high to rise. Keep your eyes on the prize, return to family/love peace and contentment. Sabir (Patience) is also rewarding. Time is constant (Go seconds to each minute). Conditions/situations cause time to appear to be long or short. Keep your mind on goals and family. Family is the glue that holds (binds)! Call if U can. Idriis Bilaal "Sweet P"

Post card sent from New Orleans on 8/19/09

Café Du Monde means Café of the World en Fracais (in French) Parle vovs Fracais (Do you speak French?) Oui (yes), or, "un porte' (a little) Languages from around the world. Easy, when U R interested. Later!

"Sweet P"

Post card sent from New Orleans on 8/21/09

Great times experienced in the "Big Easy" say so-
Krumbz, Right though it's tight. Each second closes
the time, hit will soon B over!

"Sweet P" Idriis Bilaal

8/21/09

In the name of Allah (God), the beneficent, the merciful. All praises is due to (belong) to Allah, the Lord of all the worlds of knowledge. Received 2 letters from you, happy to hear that U R doing well, physically, the mental and spiritual parts come in the morning. From the Bible Psalms 30:5, "Weeping may endure for a night", but joy cometh in the morning. How long B the night? Not long, for real, force on family and he says to B experienced when morning cometh. Allah is bigger than all. Surely Allah over all things is the power. Let not your heart (mind) be troubled nor your spirit broken. Stand tall, stay strong, U have many who cares because they know U R family. Family men don't ever loose. You have a young son who is waiting to be guided aright by his father (you)!

Ramadan starts tonight (perhaps) 8/21/09 or 8/22/09, depending on the sighting of the new moon. 28-30 days of fasting. Easy when U R doing it for Allah. No water, food or sex, between sun rise and sun set for 30 days. After the sun set, one is in order to live normal lives. After 30 days, we have a big holiday called Elid Al Fitr (Holiday the Natural)-Living natural again. Eat when one chooses. But Ramadan is a glorious time for those who embrace Islam. There should B some persons at Jessup who observe Ramadan. They observed it in the late 80's when I was teaching there.

Don't forget; remember joy comes in the morning, after the rain (storm) comes sunshine. How long is the night? Every second brings the morning nearer. Time is constant and measured in seconds. 60/minute, 3600sec per hour, 3600x24=sec/day 1. That numberx7=sec per week. And so on etc. Time is space, distant. Time should B used to enhance the minds of people. Waste no time, study, study, study, then study. Do U have access to internet? Most knowledge is or may/can B found on internet. Read, read, and read! Read your way up (to the top) and don't stop. Aim for the moon and if U miss, at least U could end up among the stars. What price da Krumbz? Hit do what hit do! The creator is bigger

Idriis Bilaal "Sweet p"
Allahu Akbaru

8/22/09

Krumbz?
Study History, the history (his story) or Mesopotamia, now, one need to study geography-geography along with history U can read about Mesopotamia, Persia, Kush, Canaan, Anatolia.
Ok, Mesopotamia is Iraq, Persia=Iran, Iran. Kush is Ethiopia, Anatolia=is Turkey, Canaan is Palestine (Isariel) Isrial from the Bible, why was Israel called the "Land of Canaan"? History again, biblical history, Noah had 3 sons, Shem, Ham, and Genesis 9:19 9:22 name father of Canaan. The other son Ja'pheth. Ham, they say was black, so or what about his son Canaan, who founded or established the land called Canaan, the people were called the "Canaanites" that's who Joshua led, the people of Israel to take the land from the Canaanites, Ham descendants had to B black. And black people worship Josh way for defeating the, or taking away the Canaanites land. Read Exodus in the Bible. Learn who the Canaanites were and still are. They R us. What is a Gentile? (Who) Krumbz? The Bible Act 16:10 Macedonia, where is this? Macedonia is Greece! So U C, one needs to study both history and geography, to know what places are called today.

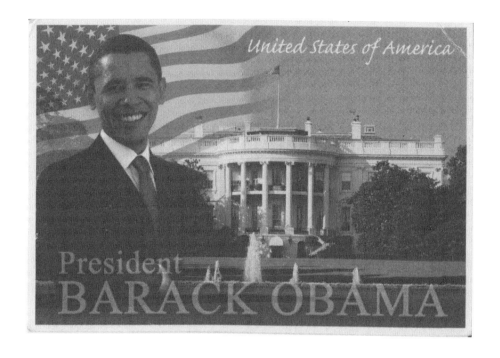

Post card sent from unknown location on 8/23/09 2nd day of Ramadan. Easy living for Allah, fasting is very beneficial for the soul (mind) What price da Krimbz? Hit do what hit do! Stay strong, joy comes in the morning. Nights (troubled times) R shorter than the days (good times). Hang on in there.

"Sweet P"
Idriis Bilaal

8/26/09

Krumbz? "Sweet P"
To: Grady McCain
In the name of Allah (God) the most beneficial, the most merciful. 'u is up 'u 'u up Grady 4:15am Wed. 8/26/09 Ramadan Mubaarik (Blessed Ramadan) Ramadan, the 9th month of the Muslim (Islamic) Calendar, is also the month in which Prophet Muhammad received the 1st verses (signs) of the Quran. You will find those 1st verses in Chapter 96 of the Quran. All Praises are due to Allah for the Honorable Elijah Muhammad, who excited the American community to Al Islam. We are in Ramadan presently (4th day), It's very spiritually beneficial to all who participate. Nothing is compulsive in Al Islam, Islam is a way of life in which it is taught that this or that is perhaps the better way to do something, not that it is the only way. One has a choice. Received a letter from U today. Glad to hear U R staying strong. 60 sec to each min 60x60 sec's in each hr. 60x60=3600 sec to the hour. Aka 3600x24=sec's/day. Remain strong! a.k.a. (also known as) What price da Krumbz? Hit do what hit do!

"Sweet P"
Idriis Bilaal

8/27/09

Our future may lie beyond our vision. We should endeavor to keep it (the future) within control. How? By keeping the creator first in all that we think or do. Next to the creator (Allah) comes family. Allah blesses those among us who do family. Who care as U do, therefore, U have a future, time-let not time B an enemy to U. Shaitaam (the Devil) is a liar, that's that! B not defeated by men or time. Allah Akbar (is bigger) and has power over all things. Human or not so human, U dig? Allahu Akbaru God is bigger

Idriis "Sweet P"

8/27/09

In the name of God the most beneficent, the most merciful, As Salaam Alaikam. (One person)

I am enjoying a book entitled, "Catching Fire", "How cooking made us human" might frighten, some might enlighten, and some might even cause some to think. The writer (Richard Wrangham) says, "Thru (evolution) we, after acquiring knowledge concerning fire, we by cooking meat developed at a faster rate than other species (apes). Our brains included. There for we are more intelligent, proof we can subdue them (other apes, and animals) Think! What price da Krumbz? Hit do what hit do!

Idriis "Sweet P"

8/30/09

In the name of Allah, the most beneficent, the most merciful.

Greetings, bro Grady, and May Allah (God) ever smile upon U and your family. I trust that most is well with U. Today is the 9th day of the 9th month (Ramadan) in/on the Islamic calendar. As U know, we fast (no eat/drink) from sun up until sun down. We start at (around) 5am and "Break" "Fast" (Breakfast) at today 7:42pm. It's easy when one knows or appreciates the purpose. Fasting indicates discipline. Can one obey? Obedience is next to Godliness. If we can not obey, parents and or those appointed over, whom we can see, how much more difficult it is to obey God, whom we cannot see (the unseen)

Ramadan-the word means, "Hot Burning", maybe with thirst or hunger, or other pleasure (sex, etc). So we restrain from these things for the sake or to obey God. Our rewards come in many ways; to many to count. We must first obey our parents, then God, then those appointed over us. Joy comes in the morning, how long is the night? The night can be considered the time of our youth, the time incarcerated (locked down). But all nights end, and Joy follows. Patience is rewarding, especially when one has 9 loving waiting family and friends waiting for the morning also.
Peace/Krumbz
Idriis "Sweet P"

8/30/09

Let not your mind be troubled. You have a great cause to survive this and be restored to society.

Your cuz, Lady C (Cheryl), called today, on her way to church that she always goes, that positive (+) A Big +, + for God (Allah). One God, one church, one Baptism, one heaven, everyone wants to go, no one wants to die. One need not die to be in a heavenly state (Peace is heaven). Having a nice family is Heaven, Kids Wife etc.

What price da Krumbz? Hit do what hit do. TRUST! Time for Salaut (Prayer) I will be going to the Mosque now, dig U later, like a sweet potato. Take is easy-

"Sweet P" Idriis

8/31/09

With the name of Allah (God), the beneficent, the most merciful. All praises are due to Him, the Creator of all things above, on, beneath, under, around, near the Earth and Universe, with his or in his name, we have our being, and therefore should give all praises to him.

My, my, my, eight months of this year has passed. How are U today, my brother? Life is well; we hope and pray for U and your family. U know the greatest or best blessing one (a male) can receive, is to be blessed to reproduce himself (another male), a son (direct). I, myself was blessed with 3 sons however, they came through my daughter. The praise be to God (Allah). You were blessed to have a direct son. Praise God some more. Shukaran/Thanks

Allah. Thank you Allah. The Creator cannot be over praised, the best thing we can do, in this life, is to praise God (Allah). He is worthy of all praise.

Study the word of Allah (God) in any and all forms i.e. Bible, Quran, Turah (Jewish), Hindu (Budah). The WORD! WORD is what matters. It's the same (on same pale) of all people; we should learn how to capture the ideas of other minds. What then is mind? Man means mind. Mind is the standard of a man. Authorized by Allah. Stale minds, leave alone stranded.

What price da Krumbz? Hit do what hit do!
Newness, freshness, variety; seek these, make them
companion of yours. Inventions are brought forth by
fresh minds, don't sleep too much.

Krumbz come to those who sleep (too much). Good
thoughts come during darkness, quietness.
Learn study, learn, listen, learn, study, and listen.
Listeners Learn! C U

Idriis "Sweet P"

Post card sent from Jamaica on 9/5/09

Greeting from Jamaica! Lovely weather. Hope U R
well. Stay strong. Joy comes in the morning. Hope to B
back soon. Looking forward to C-ing U soon.
Remembering U is all our prayers Ramadan
MURARIQS MUBARIK Blessed Ramadan.
Idriis "Sweet P"

Post card sent from S.C. on 9/11/09

Hi Grady, moving through S.C. in route to the Big Easy New Orleans. Stay strong, joy will surely come in the morning. C U, hopefully soon.

"Sweet P" Idriis

9/16/09

Hey Grady,
Peace and happiness, as better it can be experienced.
God, family, country, Allah (church), God, family.
Order of concerns. Never forget your offspring (kids).
Love them with all U have to give. Hope U realize that
every day! God is good always…

Post card sent from New Orleans on 9/17/09

Peace, strength, focus, make'em all your friends.
9/17/09. All is well with me, hope same for U!
Remain strong.

"Sweet P"

Post card from New Orleans 9/19/09

Hi Grady,
Peace, happiness, strength, endurance. May God bless
U with all of the above.

Idriis "Sweet P"

Post card sent from New Orleans on 9/19/09

Hi Grady,
Sweet P Having a boss time! We are (Cuz) in the Big
Easy. Stay strong!

"Sweet P"

9/22/09

In the name of Allah (God) I write.

Peace to U Mr. Grady (father of 7) (one new born son). I trust that your day to day is well. In fact, if U R able to read this script, U R well. Allah (God) is good, all the time. We should have nothing to bother us. What price da Krumbz? Hit do what hit do! Chill, all is not marked (over), there is so much more to your young life. Valleys come, mountains appear after. Wait on the Lord. Diamonds come from pressure/heat. Keep focused on family, that's what's up, that's your future. Long is the day, short the night, tight but right.

I'm presently in the Big Easy (New Orleans). They had it rough here. 4 years later, some R still going through tough times, we try to help, but that's all we can do, each one gives as one can. In Islam we R taught to give what is above our needs. What price da Krumbz? Hit do what hit do. I've met some brothers here in the 7th Ward (Gentilly Ave) near Dillard University, near, in fact, across the Fair Grounds and now I R one. ("I" "R" one) means, "I am presently experiencing it or living it). U dig? 'Up, datz (whatz up) Weather cool (beautiful) here around 80-85 daily, AC everywhere, so no sweat. It's 5am and I'm awake on vacation. There is no vacation from Allah's work. U don't need or desire one. Later!

"Sweet P" Idriis

9/26/09

Peace, blessings, Detroit just scored a touchdown. I returned from N.O. The Big Easy (Big E) Thursday, 8pm. About 30 hrs drive from N.O. with a one night stay in Fort Mill, S.C., 30 miles south of Charlotte, N.C. So I need to rest a little. (2 days) Now I'm ready to go again. Things went well in the Big E, little fine, no sweat. Hope to return soon. I've adopted N.O. as a second home, root for the Saints and the Hornets. Visit as often as I can to help their economy just a little, how so ever, if each or many do a little, great things can be accomplished. Allahu AKBARU. What price da Krumbz? Hit do what hit do. So I feel good about N'O Leans. Received two letters from you today, one from Cheryl, the other straight thru the mail. U seem to be holding a strong posture, which is good and necessary. U R right, it's only temporary and with your family as a focus, U can and will make it. Allah God is with those who show love for family. Don't let anyone cause U to violate any regulations of the institution. When U return, a job is the way to go. Be Legit, legal, tight but Right! U will be able to teach your young son the correct way to go. Learn all U can. Just learned that I can visit U. CALL ME, LET ME KNOW the BEST DAY and time. Being retired I can come any time, I could have come today, but I didn't get the letter until 12noon Sunday. Can visits be made

on the Weekdays? And if so, what time? Call me if U can, Hope to return to N.O. by
Sunday 2nd of October 09 for the Jets/Saints game. Hope to visit U before I go. Stay strong.

"Sweet P" Idriis

10/7/09

Received your letter of 10/3/09. I didn't make the Jets/Saints game. Was in S.C., Fort Mills, SC near Charlotte, NC.
Hope to go to N.O. for the Giants/Saints game 6th week 10/19/09. Saints could very Easy or likely go to the Super Bowl.
Later/Peace/Strength

"Sweet P"

R U able to buy stamps from your funds in the institution?
Later/Gone

10/8/09

Thursday 6am
Peace, Love, Seek Knowledge, seek her, she is worthy of the time spent in search of her. Make her (knowledge) a companion of yours. Then understanding. Knowledge w/o understanding is vanity (nothing), only the selected shall understand. When one understands, then he must pass it on to his SON. (Sun) his sun, which shines, show your light through the teachings U pass to your sun (son) La mim shoice/choice

French for "the same thing" Son=Sun, vice versa, criss cross. Like dat!

My journey to Calif (Cali) and back and subsequence trips was/is in search of Fresh mind or minds. Found few, not many, (2) I think. This doesn't mean U leave other minds behind-NO, Let no mind B left behind. (Nice Saying) but most minds, or at least some, must B left behind or hell is a lie. Further, there must B some behind in order to know where front (Good) Is. U dig? I ain't trying to lv U behind! (smiles) Later!

Sweet P (SP)

Post card sent from New Orleans on 10/8/09

Greetings dear brother, I got a feeling ALL will be well in the end stay strong and hang on in there. Think family. God, Allah will make it alright. He blesses the family man, that U R. I'm, in rout to Florida for 3 days. C U soon!

Idriis "Sweet P"

10/8/09

In the name of God (Allah) the Most Beneficent, the Most Merciful, All praises are due to Allah, Allah the Lord of all the worlds of Knowledge. In all thy getting's get (Seek) understanding, Knowledge w/o understanding is vanity, nothing (no-thing). Not a thing! Only those of understanding (comprehension) shall prosper.

Prosper; Wisdom is the proper use of obtained Knowledge. Will we learn? What price da Krumbz? Hit do what hit do.
I've been on the move much of late, I'm an air sign (Aquarius) , and like the wind, most circulate. (Go around). Move. Miles Davis (Trumpet player), plays a tune called "Move", written by Tadd Dameron (piano player) from the Day (Back in the) Jazz. Do U get to listen to Jazz (WPFW)? I think you said U do or did. I'm listening to WPFW presently. Krumbz? Krumbz

When will we Act? C.S. (Teach) CS (Common Sense). A degree is CS, all should have. Better than a PHD. What price da Krumbz? Hit do what hit do.

Hope your family is doing well. Allah will provide, thru people. God works blessings thru people or his creations.

Peace, Idriis "Sweet P"   Be of Good Cheer

10/10/09

Life is fair. People may not B. Only God can Judge, for sure and eventually (at the end) conclusion. The Judge (final) is God. B good to family, especially offspring, your future. That little boy of yours, carrier of the McCain name he is!

As Salaam Alaikam
Out/gone
S P

"Sweet P" S P
Idriis

10/11/09

Hey Grady, its Sunday morning, your cuz and I are spending a day or so in Kissimmee Florida near Orlando, time share invite taking a look, see if we like, I drove here, she flew. She's leaving the 12th of Nov. 09, I leave Monday also, but hopefully, I'll B driving. Hope things are getting more bearable for U, considering your conditions. Your future is outside and/but U must wiggle thru the valley of discomfort, joy comes in the morning, yet how long is the night, NOT LONG! Only as long as one's mind lets it B. U C, night is a period of darkness, cloudiness, gloom, and then BOOM!!!! Joy (morning), then we laugh at the night through reminiscing (Remembering), going over our lives. What price da Krumbz? Hit do what hit do.

Weather quite warm here, Tuesday forecast to reach 93degrees. That's 12/13 Oct.

Well, as previously remarked upon, every second clicked off, is a second taken, subtracted from the length of the night. Ever closer to the day when U can B with your family. We know how important that is for U. Allah is bigger than any situation. Give him praise as due. Wake up screaming (Joy), Joy, and Joy! Let not situations of this short life deter us from our roles, goals. Krumbz! Continuing, Sunday morning we R to look at a sample today. Your cuz is a joy to B around. Very good friend and companion. Later!

"Sweet P" (Idriis)

Post card sent form N.C. on 10/17/09

Hi Grady-Travel Should B more than just going from
A-B. Travel should welcome new horizons, education,
widen knowledge. I try to make it thus. Just moving on
through N.C. in route to? Right!!! Just moving on.
Take care and stay strong.
Later/gone, P" Idriis

10/17/09

In God's name we write
Dear Grady,
Life is a merry-go-round, circle, Life Circles its self, we circle ourselves, nothing new "under the son/sun". What is has been, what is to come, was. Who can find a virtuous woman? She is the glory or the crown of her husband. Should (if) she would/should make him ashamed, is the same as the rottenness to his bones. What price da Krumbz? Hit do what hit do. Continue to seek knowledge until the grave. Worry not about wisdom, seek knowledge, learn, learn, and then learn!!! The learned proper. Learned proper. God must be the number one focus. God (1), family (2), Community (3).

Received a letter from U today. Glad to C U R getting stronger. In God we trust, all others pay cash. Krumbz? Strength is first generated in the mind. Mind is the standard (measurement) of a man. He is as good/high as his mind has been elevated to. Woman made to (for the sake) of man, comfort him, not to control him. Man must B in control regardless of conditions. No exceptions! Won't work otherwise. God ordained man, Adam was 1st then Eve. Eve, Evil! Eve, careful. Lots of similarities. Krumbz? When is a good time or day to visit U? I'm in and out of town frequently lately, but give me some idea.
Later, "S-P" The "P" Idriis

10/17/09

inna Allahu alaa Kulli Shain (surely God over ALL things)
Qadir has power (is the power). A brighter day ahead for those of strong faith. SABIR patience, it will B over.

God (Allah) is good all the time. He is merciful and forgiving, and he causes society to forgive others.

Joy comes in the morning! How long is the night? Krumbz?
I have known Rivers, I know Lakes. All Rivers flow to the sea, yet the sea never over flows-WHY?
Circles…Think, focus, grow!

"P"

10/20/09

As Salaam Alaikum,
How R U today? Received a correspondence from U today. Great Spirit, that's the correct posture. Life is a bitch, and then U die, die from what? Should B from ignorance and being uniformed. Don't be of the unlearned, Learn, Learn, and then Learn!!! U will never know enough! There will always be more to learn. What price da Krumbz? Hit do what hit do. Let not a day go by without learning something U did not yesterday. Make knowledge a companion, buddy. Walk with it, her, him (knowledge). Check out your mind... Krumbz?

Had very enjoyable stay in Florida, 95 degrees. But home is home! Nothing is like home and family, as U well know. Your own family awaits your soon return. Keep hope alive and pray regularly, which is constantly, every moment you can, B praying. Work for Allah (God) is prayer, duty. Dutifully? Whenever gloom appears, think of your family, how every second that passes during the day brings you closer back to your family. 1 second closer. Your time isn't long. This too shall pass –B gone. Freedom is just around the corner, let nothing cause you U to go off the tracks that will bring U back to your little boy and your girls. Hang on in there and be strong, stay so!

Later, "P"

10/22/09

Salam, (Peace Grady)
In the name of God (Allah) the creator. Hit depends
on what the definition of it is. In order for a word to
have a definition, at least two individuals must agree
on it, the definition, (or how) the word is defined,
inSha Allah, God willing.

No mind should B left behind, but will! We hope U R
not in the company of any that could B left behind.
We are sure U will not B among them, Krumbz?
(What?) Not code! Common sense (C.S.), everyone
should obtain (earn) a degree in C.S. Don't say fuck it!!
Who shall B able to pass (test) before the great one
(God)? Who is this of whom we speak? This is God!

How will U know or recognize God? If the question
was put to me, I would think on it, then think on it
some more. Then think on it again, Prey, then wait on
an answer. Which I already know. Next episode! Stay
tuned!

Returned from Durham, NC, Greensboro and
Winston-Salem(S L M), Salim (S L M), Salem (S L M)
Peace!
Wars are always being fought about the city of Peace,
Why??? Bring to mind, what is Peace? Cain/Abel,
Adam/Eve, Adam/EVIL (same) Krumbz?
Gone, "P" Idriis

10/24/09

Hi Grady,
Just talked to your cuz; she says that I can come to C U now. So I am looking at maybe October 27th, 28th, and 29th. I know most of the directions, BWI 295 to 175 Jessup, that's it. Hope to C U between October 24-31. Having direct TV put in the house here today. Not much on watching TV except Football, Basketball, History & weather channel. But my daughters come over sometimes, even when I am out of the City. I have a 29, 19, 2 daughters and 3 grandsons, Idriis, Siddiq and Saide. 10, 6 and a 1 year old. So I know how much U miss your son. He is the Sun, the one that shines. Howard has home coming today, big parade, party, etc. Next week and Halloween, wow!!! Better things to do, Krumbz?

Do U have stamps? Seems small, nut can B important. Did U do something to raise your mind today? You should elevate the mind each and every day. What price da Krumbz? Hit do what hit do. Speak Truth to the youth! They have the future. Into their hands it must fall (faith) (future) That's what's up!

Later, "P"
MAINTAIN!

10/28/09

In the name of God, Greetings friend, a word from
Allah, the Lord, God, let not any one or circumstance,
devise your spirit. Devise-to alter from the straightway,
the way of God. The intent is very important, what did
you, I, or others intend to do. Your intentions, I'm
sure was to provide for your family, God knows.
Blessed is he who considers the poor, the imprisoned
(in prison) (jailed), those incarcerated for whatever
reason, the sick, shut-in, the handicap, etc. B kind and
U'll find joy, happiness, contentment, peace. Smile
even if U think it hurts. Just smile even at yourself, to
yourself. Krumbz? What price da Krumbz? Hit do
what hit do.

Wednesday 10/28/09, rainy, but joy will bring flowers
in the spring. Water needed by every living thing. The
last words my mother said to me were, "Bring me a
drink of water son". "Water", water-God is good to
provide water for his creatures, all of them. Water is
necessary, so is the wind, who can count the wind?
Not I! Maybe thy. Who then can capture the wind? In
February the wind comes to remove the leaves that did
not fall off the trees themselves. Note the seasons,
each bring its own to us. Krumbz? Day and night, each
has a specific purpose. Day to gather, night to recreate,
rest (regroup), etc. you dance all night sleep all day, life
to U is just a childish play.

If there exist such a man with sufficient force, he would shake off and break through and would escape from all shit (strife). He would trample underfoot all of our formulas and spells and charms and all our laws which R against nature. The slave would rise in rebellion and B Lord over us, and then the light of natural Justice would shine forth.

Who B de man, what V de force
man=mind/force=intellect shake off-overcome (we shall) break through=shake off escape=learn to tolerate any situation

Avoid to the pressure, this too, shall pass. All (old) things become new. Patience! 60sec/min. stay strong!

Later, "P" Idriis

Post card sent from New Orleans on 11/3/09

Hi Grady, This team we got is red HOT, in the B Easy (BEASY). My stay here will B short, this time Hope U R well.

Later/gone, Bilaal

GO SAINTS!!

11/3/09

In the name of God (Hello Grady),
As Salaam Alaikum, peace unto U and all U know,
especially your family and your children etc., and more
especially your son. God bless him. Allah, God has
ordained, that we B productive. We can start by
reproducing ourselves through having children, sons
and daughters. Sons must have daughters (some one's)
to reproduce (with whom) to have children.

Then the father has a great responsibility to rear,
provide for, educate the children in association with
the mother and the community (world). That means;
feed, cloth, train, develop all of these. Train a child in
the correct way, and he/she should never/won't stray
too far from the teaching. Children should B taken to
the church or mosque (house of God) for respect
training enforcement i.e., we or the children should B
first taught at home then taken to the house of God
for respect training. If a child first respects God, the
people who teach about God, then he/she will later
and better show respect for parents, teacher, police,
authority, etc., U know. Children R (our) future.

Later, "P"

11/6/09

Peace to you,
We're leaving for the vacation today (Friday Nov. 6th),
Should B back Thursday Nov. 9th. Hope that all is well
with you. God is good all the time. Stay strong, focus
on family, every second is one second less. Feed the
mind daily, even hourly. Turn negative into positive.
Remember 2 negatives =positive. You have so much
waiting for you when it's over. 7 Reasons! I will keep
in touch.

The "P" (Sweet) Idriis

Post card sent from Miami Florida on 11/7/09
Hi Grady,
Hope all is well with U. We are enjoying Miami; leave on cruise today around 4pm stopping in Jamaica then the Cayman Islands. C U
Stay strong, "P"

Post card sent from Jamaica on 11/9/09
Greetings from Jamaica. On to the Cayman Islands
tomorrow 11/10/09. Having a wonderful time with
your cuz. Hope to B back 11/12/09. Today is Tuesday
11/10/09, arriving in the Cayman Islands. Spend 1
day, back at 5pm. Then on to Miami Florida. 2 more
nights on the water, arriving in Florida Thursday
morning at 8am. C U Later, "P" All is well!

Peaceful End, Grand Cayman Islands, B.W.I.   *Photo: Tuyla Bellefleur*

Post card sent from the Cayman Islands on 11/18/09

Greetings,
From, as U C, the Cayman Islands, British West
Indies. Spent a few hours here and there. Nice place,
rich atmosphere, unlike Jamaica. Hope all is well. C U
soon

Idriis "Sweet P"

11/21/09

Greetings Grady, Dear friend
As Salaam Alaikum (Peace to you) Saturday 6am, just moving around the house getting ready to visit the Big Easy, hopefully next Tuesday November 24th or so.

Hope U R feeling well and doing well. I have been on the move a lot lately. The cruise, Memphis, etc. That's my forte' I guess. Taking truth to the youth. Trying to awaken in the youth that which, could, or may help them through. As previously stated the youth are our future. Family is very important. Off springs must be guided in the best way of life.

Each time I write U I realize that your night is shorter than before. Forget not that joy comes after the night (in the morning). What price da Krumbz? Hit do what hit do.

Not much to convey at this moment, so we will close for now. Maybe something more will come to mind before this letter is posted.

C ya, "P"

11/21/09

Received your Thanksgiving card/notes, thank U, yes
we returned safely. And I've been to Memphis and
returned. Hoping to go to N.O. next Tuesday. May be
repeating some things. However, very happy to hear U
R still focused on your goals, family first, God really
first then family! Hope to C U soon.

Your friend, "Sweet P"

11/22/09

Peace "As Salaam Alaikum" brother Grady,
Wisdom, who would know? Wisdom, what is it,
experience?
Another day, 11/30/09 still in the Big Easy, N.O.

Monday 11/30/09. Pat day for many. Big day today,
Saints play the Pats (N.E.) What price da Krumbz? Hit
do what hit do.
We cannot say too much, how important it is to stay
strong, regardless of our situation; your situation is the
shape you are in (U.R.N.). This as all other situations
shall pass. Joy will be there in the morning. How long
is the night? Not long. For our stay on earth is but a
second compared to the age of the Earth and its
Creator, Allah (God), Jesus, by any name the Creator is
the Creator and is ONE. Bless him at all times. He will
deliver U/us, and make peace and be a companion.
Krumbz?
Bad times can B used to strengthen us. As in the Gym,
more weight, more muscles. We should strive to
strengthen our minds, and that's with knowledge. All
unhappiness can B conquered through knowledge. We
benefit by applying our minds to knowledge (the
acquisition of knowledge), therefore, hold on to the
unchanging force, "God". Pray and B thankful for
even life.

Later, "Sweet P" Idriis (P)

11/30/09

Peace dear friend,
I'm still in the Big Easy (N.O.). Went to the Bayou Classic Football Game Sat. 11/28/09, Grambling won by a few points, but it was about bragging rights. Doug William, Washington's former QB went to Grambling. The other team was Southern U. Both teams are L.A. Rivalries, U know.

Monday night 11/30/09 the Saints will play the N.E. Pats. It's like Super Bowl time here. Big celebration flags everywhere. More than Dallas and Skins. So we'll C how that comes out.
God willing, I sort of plan to leave for Memphis 12/1/09. Not sure. I move by the spiritual inspirations. I keep close touch with family, my 2 daughters and 3 grandsons. Like U, I care a lot for my family.

Hope U R faring well. Shorter than when I last wrote U. Maintain strength for your family's sake. Your son and your your daughters.

Let nothing deter U from your mission to raise your children, (provide for and raise). They are your future, our future, so we must train (guide) them well in the way they should go. Krumbz?

Later, "P"

12/2/09

Nice way of keeping score!!! Hi friend Grady,
Hope all is well today. Another day that the Creator
(Lord) has allowed us to enjoy, whatever B the
situations (sits). Krumbz? Happiness, Peace,
Contentment, and joy come in the morning. How long
is the night? Short, compared to what?

Money, wealth above ones needs and that of his family
is just a nice way of keeping score. Score of what?
How much better I feel (the individual) feels above the
rest. Who is the rest? Krumbz?
TV reporting BAD weather today in N'all Leans, Big
Easy. How can God bring BAD weather? Maybe hit is
just what is needed, in His plan. Better sometimes to
tear down (destroy) in order to bring back better. Die
that you may live. Who has lived? What is living? Peace
under any sit's (situations). God is above all. We say
Allahu Akbaru!!! AKBARU. God is great, and He is.
Hang on to Him and strength cometh. All situations
become tolerable for a minute compared to what?
Point of reference. All is vanity, ALL is nothing, for
we can start (create) nothing, therefore all things
(creatures, people) R not what sustains us, God does.
Loose not Him. He softens all pain. He helps us
through our mistakes, if any we have made. Krumbz?

Brother "Sweet P" Idriis

12/6/09

3am Sunday God is ABOVE all
Peace dear friend,
Just returned from the Big Easy. Who DAT! Received a letter from U. SAD in a way, can and should be converted to positivity. Like your decision to B a real MAN and to let go, that takes a real strong man. Your children R A great concern. Selfishness is a disease. Unhealthy position to B in. I feel your pain. However pain can B transferred into learning. Change brings about conflict; most people appose change, though change occurs at all times (constantly). Change is a must.

Hope for the good of your children and their mother (your wife). It's difficult to B alone. God can make a difference. U need him (God) more than ever now. This too shall pass. Life begins at 40yrs old, because it takes 40yrs to learn how to live. One may have some slight knowledge or idea about living 70yrs. 70yrs, 3 scores and 10yrs=70yrs. Just learning to live, most people are ready to pass on, "not me"!

I hope and pray for U and your family. Don't give up; allow space for your children's mother. All is not necessarily lost. The mother may just need her space or some space for a minute. Sometimes giving space can B rewarding in a relationship between people.

Sometimes the more lenient one is with space (companion time), the less they do. They just want to know that they have their own little niche. (Corner of the universe) Fret not. Time is precious. Allow a little time; change can cause things to return to same. Your children are a great concern for both of U as parents. God gives us strength. Prey, then prey for strength. Try to rid oneself of selfishness. All animal life has a tendency to focus on self. Feel not as a lone wolf, etc. Greed/selfishness is normal for most of us (animals).

C U Later, "P"

12/11/09

Peace dear friend, wisdom helps to conquer all pain. Logic, common sense (c.s.). Can a situation B changed? If not, we must prey for the strength that is already with us to overcome situations. God has put the strength in the man (Adam) who was first, then EVE (Evil) (Live) (Devil) (Lived), play on words, message nonetheless. Krumbz?

This day, Friday 12/11/09 Juma (prey time) so I went to the Mosque. I prey to the God within me to guide me. Guidance equals door to peace. Peace under any circumstances. It makes no difference. All is vanity (nothing) and wasted in the winds of time. I hope you are experiencing an experience.

"P"

12/14/09

My friend Grady McCain,
Peace! After talking with U last evening, I sort of
became a surgeon (medicine). Surgeons do what they
must/should or taught to do to relieve pain to make
humans well or better. So it is with a spiritual surgeon,
he hurts with his logic. Logic say Adam was first
(Biblical History) then EVE or EVIL. My wife is/was
not of my blood, my children (2 daughters) R of my
loins (nuts). They R me because they R from my nuts.
If a man cannot live in peace with the woman he chose
to reproduce with, then fuck her, move on, but
provide for your offspring (children). Krumbz?

When you have done your best to provide for your
offspring and their mother, and the mother
approaches U in such a manner, one has to have the
balls and say, "FUCK-HER", my children matter.
Strong matters! When U were born, 9 females were
born at the same second; therefore, there is at least 8
more broads for U to choose from, when free. Free
your mind. Because until U can free your mind, all of
us are not free. FREE YOUR MIND! No broad is
worthy or your tears! Your children, your children
matter.

Allah's Peace on U! "P"

12/16/09

Greetings Grady, Love, Peaces, Understanding, Strength, Stay Strong, Let Nothing Bother U. God gives the strength (more strength) to the man than to the female, B a man, B manly, "STRONG". Deal with things, whatever they B. Love, Marriage, Separation, deal with it! Sure it can B tuff, but as a man or men, we must deal with IT, whatever it B. Time removes all ills. No ill is greater than HE who provides all. Prey, lean on Him (Allah). He is greater, stronger than all of us.

Man, time is broken down into seconds. Tick them off, and soon U'll B free and hopefully B ready to resume your life with you children, especially your son. Bring him up strong. Don't let hang ups, hang U up! Krumbz? (What Price)

In a few days, 2009 will B behind (us), but Allah (God) has a recorder, keeper, YOU!!! U know what U had intended to do. Allah, God, judges on our intent, what were we (you) trying to do? So U, I, failed. The intent is taken into consideration by Allah. Let not yourself B bothered by neither men nor women. Women R our help, meet not our main focus. The most important focus in our short life should B over children, and more important, our grandchildren, when they come. Stay focused and strong. B a giant!

Later, "P"

Post card sent from Alabama on 12/24/09

I'm sending this a little late, it got lost. Been dere stood dere, Krumbz? Allah Akbaru, God is great! Stay strong and focused.

Idriis

Post card sent from Charlotte N.C. on 12/24/09

Hi my friend, God is still good. I'm on the move, but U R not forgotten, hang tuff. This too shall pass. Stay strong for your son/daughters.

"Sweet P"

12/30/09

Peace my dear friend Grady,
I've been on the move, N.O., Atlanta, S.C., Charlotte,
etc. I have not forgotten a friend and a most dedicated
father. Year almost over (09), New Year, new decade,
time for new ideas. Hopefully it will be the year U
return to your Lovely children and their mother, your
wife. I pray for that. B of courage. For those into God,
all occurrences are of good. Even incarceration, Paul
(bible) was in jail, Mandela (27yrs), and then became
president of South Africa MLK. So confinement
marks not the end of a good mind. It's time to repair
(the mind), bring about change. Change in how we do
things i.e. support our family.

Be strong; call whenever you can, hope I am at home.
Will visit soon I hope. Leaving soon for S.C. (New
Year) Write if U get word.

Peace/Love
"Sweet P" Idriis

1/19/10

The letters he is referring to is on pgs. 67 & 68

Dear friend (Grady),
This is a note of communication I wrote to U when I first heard of your problem with your spouse (wife). I thought it was a bit strong, so I did not send it to U. Now that strength has come to U, now is the time, digest it, it is surgery! Krumbz?

"P"

1/27/10

Peace to you dear friend,
Life is a Bitch, and then U die. Hold on to life. Your
offspring are your life. Man produces corn, wheat, etc
through the earth (ground), he harvests, not the
ground, but more corn, wheat, children, grand
children, not the ground through which they came, or
were produced. Krumbz? Shit! BS. Truth is what U
should seek, seek the truth then freedom is yours,
wherever or whatever situation one is in. Incarceration
is temporary if one makes it so. Let not your mind
(soul) be incarcerated, by neither man nor woman.
Krumbz? Adam was 1st then EVE or EVIL. EVE is
given to Adam (man) as a helper and more over a
TESTER. Tester of man's strength, Samson/Delilah
(parable).

I am happy to feel the growth of your strength. Keep
growing. Shed tears, let it B for your offspring, your
son, your name carrier. EVE doesn't carry your name
or your traits. (Blood) does dat.
The Who Datters won (Saints), big thing in the Big
Easy (New Orleans) I considering rolling down to
Miami (Super Bowl) in Sha Allah (good) God willing.
Good Lord willing and the creek don't rise. 1/27/10
Halt for a minute.

Stay strong, "Sweet P" Idriis

2/6/10 Sat. (Snowing)

God is good-
Hello or Salam (Peace) dear friend. Live, give of self buys a reward from God. Keep God first, all other will follow.

Who Dat, say dey gonna beat dem Saints? No one! Krumbz? Think, be strong. Rome not built in a day. All things good or bad shall pass. Wait, be of stout stuff. Been there done dat. If God allows it, on the 14th of Feb. 2010, I will have been around the sun 83 times. That's what age is. If the earth rotates on its axis in 28 days, on the 29th day begins a new month. Then why some months have 30, 31, 28, days? Think, Explore…

Idriis "Sweet P"

Praising you for your new instant Karen. Hell man, life is what U cause it to B for U. When U or I were born, 8-10 females were also born at the same second. Birth ratio (male/female). So how can or does a man appear tearing (crying) over one. God has made it necessary for a/each male to entertain intercourse with at least 6-9 females in order for females to B in position to do what they are in existence for "help meet". Cry not, move on to another. The right one is/has been provided. Focus on your offspring (your son, etc)

"Sweet P"

2/6/10

Love, peace my friend, I wish U well and strength. I felt your strength in your last letter. That's it, dat shit, this life is what we, (you) cause it to B. For U. Let no man/woman dictate life for U. Only God can dictate your life with your cooperation. God is good and just.

Adam was first, then EVE, who is EVE? Krumbz? Price. Answer. Rhetorical. Back to U. Answer it yourself. Parable, example, superstition. Suppose. If, Think!!! Employ your mind, explore. Learn. Understand. Live then give. Give to live. Don't have money, give U, self. God created us to assist each other, regardless to our situation (sit).

Glad, really happy to feel your strength, under your situation (sit), strengthens me. You are young (39), baby, beginning of life (40). Shed not one tear for the situation. Cry (tears) of joy for discovering who is with U. Ben there done dat. This too shall pass, (All) time measured in seconds. Count! Learn, this will B over.

Love, Idriis "Sweet P"
I will B 83 14 Feb. 10 in Sha Allah if it's God's will.
(Just a number)

Post card sent from N.O. on 2/19/10

Greetings (Peace) from the Big Easy. Hope all is well.
Saints went marching in. B encouraged, B strong. This
too shall pass. I'll write more when I get back.

Peace out, "Sweet P"

2/28/10

Peace /Blessings
Greetings dear friend Grady,

Back in DC again, lots of snow U know. Hope the snow and other things are not holding nor retarding your development. Paul was in, Mandela was in. Being in can offer an opportunity to advance how we think. Time to B still, tight but right! Meditate; listen to your spirit which is from God. Redo self; maybe 1st choice was not it. Never brewed over the action of EVE, She's EVE, (EVIL) check-mate! Adam was first, then EVE, peripheral (Rib) not a bone, but likeness of a man. No-without testicles. (holes) to be filled. Krumbz? Help meet, if not helping even opposing or unfaithful-F-them. Move on. 8-1, for whenever a male born, 8 females born. Why cry over one. Tears R for bigger things, i.e. children, (you're) not the ground from which they came (their mother) your children's mother is likened unto filth, soil to plant, U reap from the soil, U don't reap the soil, corn not dirt. Focus on the corn, not from whence the children came. Man can acquire a new plantation; if/when soil is spoiled. Move on! Stop/for a min.

3/12/10

Peace and love my friend, Krumbz? Things happen inside and outside wherever U R. However life MUST go on. Your cuz and I R not doing things as before. We still dig each other, how so ever, shit happens. I'm cool, so is your cuz.

About your sit (situation), NEXT BUS!!! Hey, U miss one bus (your wife), on to another. Karen seems like a good bus for a min. Adam was 1st then EVE (EVIL), comprehend? Drop no tear on any one female. God provided many. Focus on U (your children). Ladies (females) R similar to ground (EARTH) into which a real man plants his seed after harvest, (birth of your children) the ground, earth, soil, wife, mother of children maybe no longer required, especially if the ground is disrespectful. Later baby, move on to better ground, maybe Karen. However, even with this (Karen) move cautiously with her, check it out. All that glitters is not necessarily gold.

Your children are your focus, or should B. Make your set back a set up. Change neg. to pos. U can, U must for your children. When the creator is ready to make a change in your life, HE'LL put a new person in your life. (Look for them, him, or her) evaluate thoroughly. Do right by your children, God will make it alright.

3/22/10

Peace to U my friend Grady. Fear not your future, shape it!!! Decide what your future shall B by preparing oneself today. Study, learn, listen, and learn again. Repeat not that which has failed before. Worry not about revenge. That belongs to the creator.

Focus on your children and their future. Get over shit, put it behind. You're young. Not even half through. Live for your children. Be prepared to provide for them, and educate them. That's your obligation and a cheerful acceptance. U C your children R our future. Your son carries your seed. No revenge is worthy of that sacrifice. Explore all avenues of learning.

Faith, hope, charity; the greatest of these is charity. Give to live. Giving is rewarding, even giving of self, time, etc. Stay strong, this too shall pass!

Peace, "P"

Post card sent from Florida on 4/2/10

Greetings friend, from Florida! Moving around a little. Hope U R well. Hang tuff and stand tall. It's getting shorter. C what's up!

Peace, "Sweet P" Idriis

4/9/10

Communication ~ Dat's it!
Greetings my friend, keep your eyes on the prize! Your prize is reuniting with your son, (seed) and daughters. Goal, mission, think and reflect.

I received your communication recently. See U as moving ahead. Hey!!! Your second in incarceration is just that, a second. Compare to the age of the earth (civilization). Any way the wind blows, must be/is cool to the one who needs cooling.
Success depends upon power. Power should B defined as an organized effort. Organization requires a 1st stop and that should B a definite purpose. Purpose, U C then, is always essential if one would be successful. No purpose, no success, no power. Not even brain power. (Mind)

"Sweet P"

Post card sent from N.O. on 5/3/10

Greetings my friend,

Been busy, been traveling, haven't forgotten U, hope U R doing well. This shall pass, and is passing constantly. I'm just returning from down south. Call if U can.

"Sweet P" Idriis

Post card sent from unknown location on 5/22/10

Haven't forgotten about U bro. I've just been on the
go (move). Hang on in there, you are getting short.
Time moves on. Focus on your children (future),
Krumbz? I received your last note, real nice. Hope to
C U home soon.

"Sweet P" idriis

Post card sent from San Francisco on 6/11/10

Greetings,
I'm passing through on the move. Hope U R well.
Remain strong! I haven't forgotten you. Just moving a
lot and on retreat.

Idriis

6/28/10

Peace and love. Just returned home and found your last letter. Sorry to hear about the decision concerning your parole. Suffering is always temporal, happiness can B eternal. How long is the night? Suffering=night. Stand strong, you'll find the night is considerably short compared to the day (happiness). What price da Krumbz? Hit do what hit do.

Happy to hear U saw your younglings on or around Father's Day. That can B very important, when they first say, "Da-Da" and they know what it means. /who Da-Da is, even who Ba-Ba is. (Trinidad) Grandpa. (Ba-Ba) I have a 23 month old grandson that said he knows who Ba-Ba is. I had a chance to see then all 92 daughters) and 3 grandchildren on Father's Day.

Your night 2-4 years is becoming or reaching its overness every second. Call when U get a chance.

C U, Tuff love, "Sweet P" Idriis

Post card sent from S.C. on 8/6/10

Spirit Revival from the home of S.C. slavery, my
mother's roots. I found my grandfather's grave! God is
good.
Take care,

"Sweet P" Idriis

Post card sent from Florida on 8/7/10

Greetings from out in the world. Time is moving on, not long now. Stay strong. Been on the move. Revival time. Hope U R well. Be of good courage. The night is getting shorter. How long the night?
C U,

"Sweet P" Idriis

Post card sent from Louisiana on 8/12/10

Greetings from the Easy. Life is life. Your night is
getting shorter. Stay cool and strong. Joy comes when
over. Stay focused on your son. That's your future!
C U later alligator,

"P" Idriis

Post card sent from N.O. on 8/31/10

Hi Grady,
Hope U R well. I'm still on the move. Praises be to
God, the creator. Been going to revivals etc., it keeps
me going. Be cool.
Stay strong,

"Sweet P" Idriis

Post card sent from N.C. on 9/9/10
Greetings my dear Hermano (Bro), Spanish. Mi Hermano. (My bro) I'm teaching my grandchildren a little Spanish these days. They will need it in the near future. Your son also will need to know. I'm in S.C. to search for my roots, on my mother's side. York, S.C. You are getting shorter. Patience and strength!

"Sweet P" Idriis

Post card sent from N.Y. on 9/10/10

NY. Had to run to the Apple for a minute. Same as always. Rushing Hip, and 7th Place. Hope all is as well as can be for U. U R getting short. Keep your head high. U R somebody. Focus on your son, that's U. Future. Strength lies within the mind. So feed your mind things of good (God).

Idriis "Sweet P"

9/20/10

Krumbz?
If you thank God for everything that happens to U,
nothing bad can or will ever happen to U, because U
give thanks, regardless to what occurs. Can U dig it?
God is good all the time, his kindness is always about.
I wish I could B so kind. And all others if we
could/would be kind and do justice to/by each other,
what a awesome world of experiences we could live
under any conditions. Krumbz?

I m chasing my family records, justice was denied in
some cases. What price?

They gave a tour of the historical site around Rock Hill
S.C. 30 miles south of Charlotte, N.C. My mother
came from that area. I lived there when I was near the
age of 6 to 10 years old on a farm. Much has changed
in those years since then, interesting though. I intend
to return sometime this week. 8 hours to drive.
Catch U later,

"Sweet P" Idriis

I had a few minutes to teach my grandson a little Spanish. By the time he is 18 to 20 years old (he's 12 now) he will need Spanish to be the boss pr supervisor of a company. So I admonish, advise him to take Spanish very seriously in school.

How are U my friend (brother), hope things are bearable with U. U R getting shorter each second. Keep the faith and pray for strength. It will, this too shall pass, and B yester-years (days). Keep your head/chin up, B proud of what your goal was and still is. Your offspring (children) especially your son, only one. B proud of him. Hang on in there for him. Don't let hang ups; hang U up! Krumbz?
C U later-Respect,

"Sweet P" Idriis

1) Mi Hermano=My Brother
2) Creo en Dios=I Believe in God (Allah)
3) Horas-hour
4) La=the
5) Los=the (plural) more than one
6) Voy a La biblioteca todo Los dias=I go to the library every/all the days

9/23/10

Back in S.C. in search of family roots, this can and has gotten quite interesting. This could be done at the archives bldg in D.C. or by internet, but I find it more joyous at the places where things occurred in S.C., York County, Fishing Creek School, my 1st grade school. Revisiting S.C. is like digging for roots. For me, it was about 1931-1939. Farming and doing it all…Memories!
Later,

"P"

Sacramento at Dusk

Post card sent from Sacramento on 10/13/10

Do U know who Richard Wright is?
Greetings As Salaam (Peace) Blessings. Moving on, life
is short. Got to get it while it's here. Hope your
faring/doing ok/well. Time for U is getting short. Stay
strong, hang tuff. This too shall pass, God is great,
He'll C U thru, and your son/daughters.
C U, "Sweet P" Idriis

10/26/10

Greetings from D.C. stuck in a hotel, but doing well. Hope U R ok, God is good. Keep faith, all will B good! Time is constant, in a few days we'll all B free. Free your mind first with knowledge, info, and pray for understanding. Make her (understanding) your goal. Your cuz told me what happened, DAMN!!! Krumbz? I'm doing ok, hope U R doing the same or better. I'm still moving on. I'm invited to Thanksgiving in Winston Salem N.C. by Niece and Nephew, family. Something to do. Dec. 27th, plan to B in Atlanta. Saints play the Falcons. Hang tuff. Don't let hang ups hang U up.

C U, "Sweet P" Idriis

11/13/10

Friend, B what U is, don't B what U ain't, aint what U once have been, it's what U now am is dat counts any how!

What price da Krumbz? Hit do what hit do. Hanging on Allah, God is good. His mercy is always with us. Faith and strength. Don't let hang ups hang U up.

How is your family, the pillar of us, your son, is U. We live through our sons and daughters as well. I have no known direct son; however Allah has blessed me with 3 grandsons. I shall live (always) or I could live forever through them. Therefore we must educate our sons/daughters. First about God, Allah the creator. 1st fear God, then father, then God. A 1 day old baby obeys it's mother, it doesn't know about God, then his/her father, the Allah…FEAR=RESPECT

Improve your mind and your standard. Grow your intelligence. Read, Read then Read. Internet if available. Learn and seek understanding. Understanding without understanding knowledge is vanity (nothing) VANE. All is real; expose yourself to all forms of information. Waste not your hours.

Hope your lawyers succeed. Heard about your cuz, all is well then. Not clever, but the Quran say, "the male

is not like the female, they need guidance, God put man in charge. Adam was
first, then EVE. EVE was deceived, then she misled ADAM, or

ADAM followed a misinformed female. All is well with your cuz though.

C U, "P" Idriis

3/24/11

Greetings Grady,
I've been quite involved in stuff myself lately. Fire at the house and insurance debates. Hope U R well, haven't been as involved with your cuz as much as before, we R still cool though, C her every now and then. Hope your children are well and progressing in school. I'm still living in a temp apt. address is 130 M street, N.E. Wash. DC 20002. May be there for another 2/3 months. Nice place, new Apt. 2 blocks away from my home.

Your stay there is getting shorter and I know you are ready to depart and come back to your family, they need U.

Spring has sprung; all is beginning to get green. Stay cool, fool. I know U know how to receive that.

Later, Bro Idriis Bilaal

Idriis Bilaal & Grady McCain
MCI-J 2009
"Krumbz"

Letters to inmate #355-188

ACKNOWLEDGMENTS

Letters by: Idriis Bilaal

Cover by: Nicholas Smith

nasdesign@mac.com

Foreword by: Tamika Diggs

Meeklove.lovespeaks@gmail.com

Photography by: Anthony Harding (Convict at MCI-J)

Special Thanks

Tamika Diggs for everything you have done for me since I've been out of jail as well as helping me put my first ever book together. Without you this project would have never been possible. I wish you success in all that you do!

"Belford Towers Family"

6733 North

Thank You

I would like to thank my sister Jessette McCain and my mother Vivian McCain for all the sacrifices that they have made in order to secure my well being with their time, money, and personal assets. I would also like to thank Mother Beverly (Joan Beverly) for her loving letters of encouragement and support, Larry Beverly, my brother from another mother Sherwyn Devonish, my homie and friend for life Andre Lewis, Ant Mo (Anthony Hare), Wall Street (Kevin Forrester), Smiley (Todd Smiley), Nicholas Smith, my cousin Delicia McCain Ennis for allowing me to stay with her while on house arrest, Linda S., Stephanie Harper Fields for all of the support and love she has given to me during my time of need, Jeanene "Jae" Thomas for seeing my true potential and motivating me to become all that I can be, Dionne Burkett Lewis for being such a good friend, and saving the best for last, all of my children, Zion, Zania, Ariona, Zayana, Zierra, Zaria, and Zaniqua, for being the motivation and drive in my life to be successful. For all that I missed; I got you on the next project.

R.I.P.

Robert Willie McCain Sr.

999

ON

gmacmrmac@gmail.com

krumbzletters@gmail.com

This book is dedicated

to all of my fallen soldiers and

all of my homies still doing time in

state and federal prisons.

SALUTE!

"World Inside A World"

Special shout out to "Byron (B-Bo) Dorsey"

D.C. For Life!

Courage is not the absence of fear, but rather the judgment that something is way more important than being scared. Believe you can do anything; succeed in spite of fear!

John Dough

#BESCAREDOFNOTHIN
#GIVEEVERYTHINGURBEST
#HAVETHECOURAGE2SUCCEED

Fear is a decision!

Made in the USA
Middletown, DE
08 February 2019